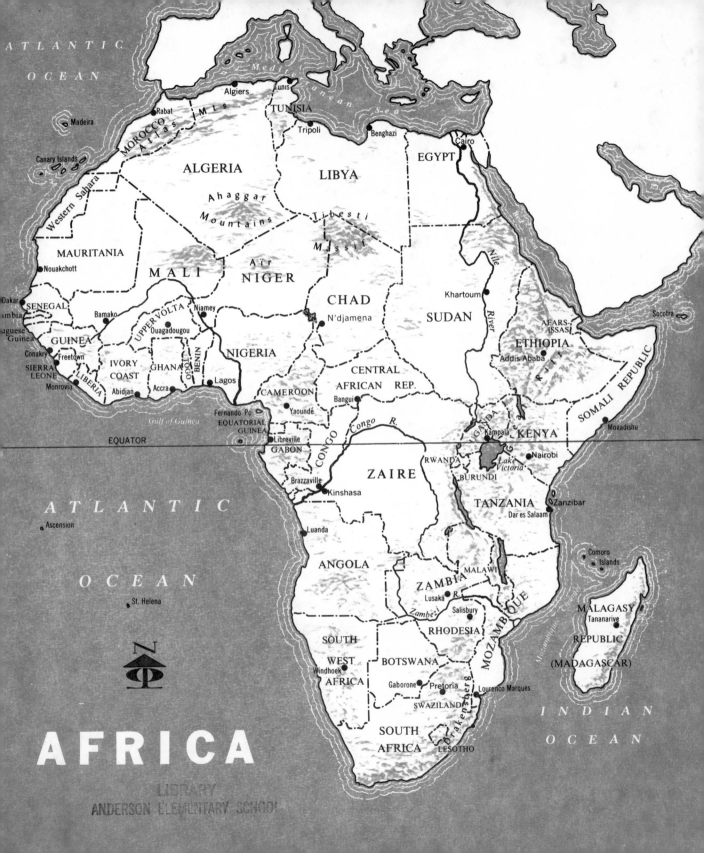

Enchantment of Africa

CAMEROON

by ALLAN CARPENTER
and JAMES HUGHES, Ph.D

Consulting Editor
John Rowe, Ph.D
African Studies Faculty
Northwestern University
Evanston, Illinois

CHILDRENS PRESS, CHICAGO

THE ENCHANTMENT OF AFRICA

Available now: Benin (Dahomey), Botswana, Burundi, Cameroon, Central African Republic, Chad, Congo (Brazzaville), Egypt, Gabon, Gambia, Ghana, Guinea, Ivory Coast, Kenya, Lesotho, Liberia, Libya, Mali, Malagasy Republic (Madagascar), Malawi, Mauritania, Morocco, Niger, Rhodesia, Rwanda, Senegal, Sierra Leone, Sudan, Swaziland, Tanzania, Togo, Tunisia, Uganda, Upper Volta, Zaïre (Congo Kinshasa), Zambia

Planned for the future: Algeria, Equatorial Guinea, Ethiopia, Nigeria, Somalia, South Africa

ACKNOWLEDGMENTS

Secretary General, Ministry of Information, Federal Republic of Cameroon, Yaounde; Embassy of the United States of America, Yaounde; Embassy of the Federal Republic of Cameroon, Washington, DC; Rev. Père Engelbert Mveng, Director of Cultural Affairs, Yaounde; Photographs and Exhibits Section, United Nations, New York

Cover: The mosque at Douala, Allan Carpenter
Frontispiece: Motorcyclist with a two-wheeled trailer passes a small refreshment stand in a town across the bay from Douala, Michael Roberts

Project Editor: Joan Downing
Assistant Editor: Elizabeth Rhein
Manuscript Editor: Janis Fortman
Map Artist: Eugene Derdeyn

LIBRARY OF CONGRESS
CATALOGING IN PUBLICATION DATA

Carpenter, John Allan, 1917-
  Cameroon.
(Enchantment of Africa)

  SUMMARY: Introduces the history, geography, culture, government, and people of an African nation along the Gulf of Guinea.
  1. Cameroon—Juvenile literature. [1. Cameroon]
I. Hughes, James, 1934- Joint author. II. Title
DT564.C35   967'.11   77-670
'SBN 0-516-04555-5

Contents

A True Story to Set the Scene

KING MANGA BELL'S PROTEST

In 1913 rumors spread rapidly among the Douala people about their German colonial neighbors. It was said that the local Germans would try to force the Douala off their homeland. Some Douala heard that the Germans were trying to take over their trading rights, too. The Douala were worried that they could lose their livelihood and ancestral homeland.

The king of the Douala, Manga Bell, listened carefully to the concerns of his people. His advisory council thought that king Manga Bell should protest the threats directly to the German colonial governor.

Soon the rumors became fact. The German colonial officials were considering plans to force the Douala to leave their homeland. Supposedly, Europeans living along the coast (in Doualaland) were fearful of malaria, yellow fever, and other indigenous (native) diseases.

The mosquito was the dreaded carrier of some of these illnesses. Europeans accused the Africans of poor sanitation practices, which they said encouraged the spread of malarial mosquitoes. Since mosquitoes rarely travel distances of more than a mile, some Europeans proposed that all Africans be moved at least one mile from Douala.

Not only would this move destroy the homeland of the Douala people, it would

Sculptures of German soldiers, located outside a house where men gather for ceremonial drinks, show how strongly the German influence was felt in colonial Cameroon.

also destroy most of their contacts with the coastal traders. The Douala feared that the Germans' motives behind such a move were more mercenary than sanitary.

When the Germans had originally signed a treaty with the Douala people in 1884, they had promised to leave all trading rights to the Douala. In suggesting that the Douala be moved, the colonial officials seemed to be breaking the treaty, as well as stealing Douala land. King Manga Bell met with the German colonial governor. The king pleaded his case and asked for reassurance that such "rumors" were false. The colonial governor, however, would make no promises.

Once again, the Douala people gathered to consider their plight. The people decided that they must send a representative to Germany to protest directly to the German emperor. People contributed what they could afford, and finally a representative left for Germany. King Manga and his people anxiously awaited a response.

King Manga had feared that the leaders in Germany might not listen to his representative. It is said that he had considered asking both the French and English governments for help if the German government refused him.

At this time in Europe, stirrings of World War I were in the air. France and England were about to ally against Germany. The German colonialists in Cameroon were not at all happy when they heard that King Manga Bell would even think of asking their European "enemies" for assistance.

When word of King Manga's action reached the colonial officers in Cameroon, it was regarded as an act of treason. King Manga Bell was arrested by the Germans for his acts. He was convicted of treason. In the summer of 1914, the king was hanged by the German colonial officers for his act of protest.

The Face of the Land

THE CHARIOT OF THE GODS

During the fifth century B.C., a Carthaginian explorer named Hanno sailed along the western coast of Africa. Along the coast of what is now Cameroon, he is said to have sighted a great, erupting volcano. In describing the awesome sight, Hanno called this mountain "the chariot of the gods."

Some historians question whether Hanno actually traveled as far along the coast

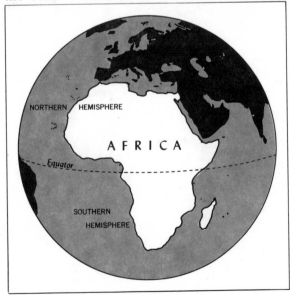

of Africa as Cameroon. Perhaps his writings have been misinterpreted. Perhaps Hanno was repeating information he had heard from others. Perhaps he did see Mount Cameroon.

Whether Hanno's stories are true is not important. If he had seen Mount Cameroon, he would certainly have been impressed. This huge mountain appears to rise out of the ocean in the Gulf of Guinea. More than thirteen thousand feet high, this mountain is not only the highest point in all of Cameroon, it is also the highest point in all of west-central Africa.

Masses of clouds often obscure the view of the mountain's summit, adding a bit of mystery to the scene. Sometimes snow settles on the mountaintop. The white, snow-capped peaks are indeed a dramatic contrast to the hot, humid jungle that nestles along the mountain's base.

Much of the cloud formation around Mount Cameroon is also unique. The clouds often condense, dropping much rain onto the mountain. The highest annual rainfall in the African continent has been recorded along the foothills of this mountain. That record rainfall was more than four hundred inches a year! (This is ten times as much rain as New York City gets.) But Mount Cameroon is only one of the many interesting and varied features of the United Republic of Cameroon.

LOCATION

Cameroon is in the west-central part of Africa, just north of the equator along the Gulf of Guinea. Because it is positioned along the coast midway between the continent's westernmost and southernmost points (Senegal and South Africa respectively), Cameroon is often referred to as "the hinge of Africa."

This triangular-shaped country has an

MAP KEY

Abong-Mbang, F4
Adamawa Plateau, D3
Atlantika Mountains,
  C4

Bafia, F3
Bamenda, E2
Banyo, D3
Batouri, F4
Benoué River, C4
Buea, F2

Cameroon Mountains,
  E1

Dja River, G4
Douala, F2

Ebolowa, G3
Edea, F2
Edea Falls, F2

Fernando Po Island
  (Equatorial
  Guinea), F1
Foumban, E2

Garoua, C3

Kadei River, F5
Kribi, F2

Lake Chad, A4
Logone River, B5

Mandara Mountains,
  B4
Maroua, B4
Mbalmayo, F3
Mount Cameroon, F2

Ngaoundere, D4
Ngoko River, G5

Nkambe, D2
Nyong River, F4

Sanaga River, F3

Tiko, F2

Victoria, F2

Waza Game Reserve,
  B5
Wouri River, F2

Yaounde, F3

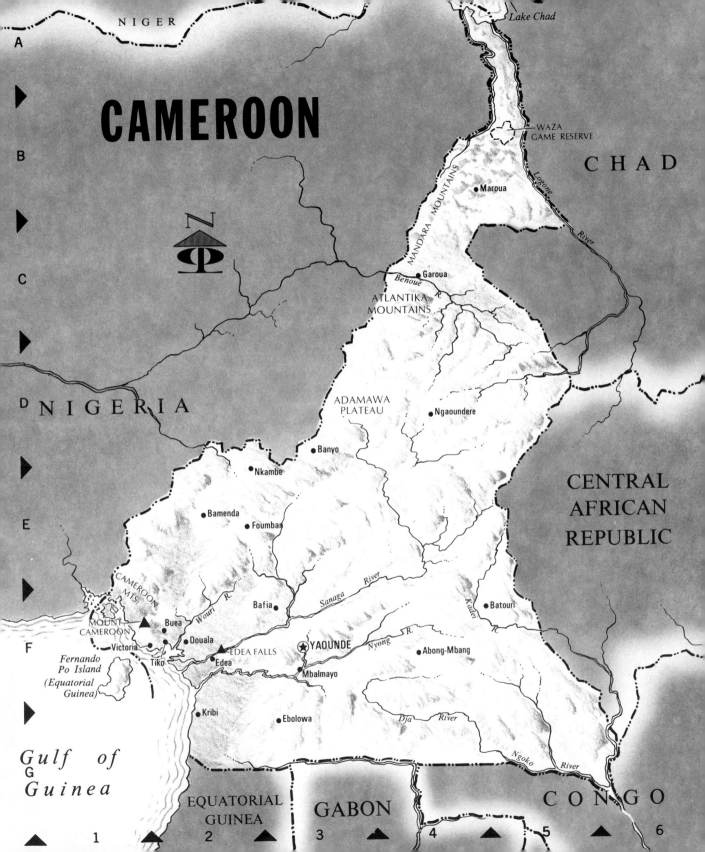

Thousands of varieties of plants thrive on the mountain slopes less than ten miles from the center of Yaounde, Cameroon's capital.

area of 183,381 square miles—about the size of California. The Gulf of Guinea lies along the country's western border. To the north lies the Republic of Nigeria, with Chad on the northeast. Directly east is the Central African Republic. Sharing the southern border (from east to west) are the People's Republic of the Congo (Brazzaville), Gabon, and Equatorial Guinea.

FIVE REGIONS OF CAMEROON

Mountains Volcanic mountains extend from the northeastern part of the country along the northern border, ending at the Gulf of Guinea. The highest mountains of this chain are the Cameroon Mountains, near the coast. Mount Cameroon is part of this range. It stands out abruptly from the other peaks, which average eight thousand feet high. The whole range stands out from the otherwise low coastal lands. Breathtaking paths and switchback roads crisscross the land from the valley floors to the mountain summits.

As this chain of mountains extends into the interior, the mountains diminish in height. In the Atlantika Mountains, which border Nigeria in the northeast, occasional volcanic outcroppings jut out of the plateau landscape. In the northern part of this chain, where the elevations are the lowest,

the Mandara Mountains reach as high as forty-seven hundred feet. The bountiful rain in the mountain chain forms numerous streams and rivers, with picturesque rapids and waterfalls flowing down the mountains and hills.

Coastal lowlands The coastal lowlands sharply contrast with the mountains. The lowlands extend for about two hundred miles along the Gulf of Guinea and inland for about forty or fifty miles.

Cameroon's many streams and rivers flow from the highlands down to the coast,

Fishermen's homes are strung along the beaches of Douala's harbor.

depositing their waters in the ocean. Vast estuaries have formed around the mouths of many of these waterways, as the silt carried from the fast-flowing waters is deposited in masses to form sandbars along the oceanfront. The Wouri River estuary at Douala is perhaps the largest of these.

In the shallow, oceanfront areas are also massive marshlands and swamps. Mangrove swamps, with lush undergrowth and tangled vegetation, make much of the lowland region almost impassable. Huge clouds of mosquitoes and other tropical insects and wildlife also keep traffic from moving through this region. In the past, the coastal swamplands earned the name "The White Man's Graveyard," because many European traders died here. Until recently, malaria, blackwater fever, and sleeping sickness were common in this area, bringing tremendous death tolls to early European settlements.

Rainfall in the coastal lowlands often reaches 150 inches a year. Temperatures average eighty degrees Fahrenheit, with relative humidity almost always 80 percent. These extremely harsh conditions are part of the reason why both Africans and Europeans often avoided settling in this part of Cameroon.

Interior lowlands The interior lowlands share many of the same characteristics as the coastal lowlands. The interior lowlands encompass much of the land south of the Sanaga River and east to the Central African Republic border. The land in this region rises slightly in elevation. Rarely, however, does the elevation exceed two thousand feet above sea level. With the Sanaga River, the Nyong, Dja, Kadei, and Ngoko rivers also drain much of this region. Other smaller streams, which form tributaries to these waterways, also meander through this heavily forested tropical area.

In this spectacular tropical rain forest, huge trees several hundred feet high form gigantic umbrellas or ceilings for the forest. Smaller trees and ferns grow beneath this upper layer. Numerous climbing vines and other assorted greenery add to the dense, dank, humid atmosphere of the tropical forest. The rainfall in this area is about sixty to eighty inches a year. Humidity is also very high. There is little variation in temperature between day and night in the rain forest.

Central plateau The central plateau is often considered the most pleasant part of Cameroon. Here the land varies in elevation from twenty-five hundred feet to five thousand feet above sea level.

The Adamawa Plateau begins where the southern lowlands end and extends northeast to the savanna region. Moderate rainfall occurs on the plateau, averaging around sixty inches of rain each year. Humidity is not extremely high. With the pla-

Located in the heart of Cameroon's interior lowlands, this village seems very remote. But slowly, contacts between the coast and villages like this one are growing.

CAMEROON MINISTRY OF INFORMATION AND TOURISM

Cameroon's lush forests yield a variety of woods.

CAMEROON MINISTRY OF INFORMATION AND TOURISM

teau's moderately high elevation, there is a comfortable change in temperature from day to night—often as much as twenty degrees in the highest areas. Throughout the plateau are lush vegetation and occasional forests.

Savanna In the northeast is the savanna. On these plains, vast animal herds once roamed freely. Elephant grass, shade trees, and other smaller shrubs and grasses still characterize this region's landscape. The Benoué River flows through the savanna and continues its journey through Nigeria to the sea. The Logone River forms the region's eastern border. It empties into Lake Chad.

16

Less rain falls in the savanna than in any of the other regions of Cameroon. The savanna is sometimes subject to seasonal dry and wet spells. Like much of the savanna lands of interior western Africa, droughts sometimes occur in this part of Cameroon. Some of this land suffered during Africa's major drought of the late 1960s and early 1970s.

CLIMATIC SEASONS

Cameroon's climate is as varied as its topography. The climate is generally characterized as being tropical. High humidity and high temperatures prevail in the lower elevations, providing for a typical tropical climate. But the high elevations of the plateau, plains, and mountains tend to moderate the climate, providing for less humidity and greater temperature range. Exten-sive rainfall occurs in most of the country.

Wet and dry seasons are characteristic of this land. Usually the dry season runs from early November to mid-May. During this season, strong northerly winds blow in from the Sahara, carrying dust and sand particles. This wind is called the *harmattan*. Then the wet, or rainy, season begins, lasting through October. During the wet season, rain is common but not constant. Overcast skies prevail, causing periodic downpours and violent thunderstorms. Hailstorms occur occasionally in the high mountain areas.

This unique combination of topographies in the Cameroon landscape—particularly its volcanic soils, together with its warm and moist climate—have produced some of the richest agricultural land in all of western Africa. It is no wonder that so many people from so many parts of the world have taken an interest in Cameroon.

MICHAEL ROBERTS

A huge tree stands guard over the marketplace at Douala. Soon Betote, Simon, and the regular merchants will arrive to sell their wares.

Three Children of Cameroon

BETOTE OF DOUALA

The first glow of the sun had just begun to light up the narrow roadways on the outskirts of Douala. Most of the people in the city were still asleep. But Betote had already been up for an hour. He was preparing for his first day of "business" at the great marketplace near the train depot in downtown Douala.

Betote's home is near the Wouri River. As soon as he woke up that morning, he walked to the river's edge and washed himself in the water. At home he put on a clean shirt and clean short pants, then ate some fresh fruit and drank milk-tea. Now Betote was ready for his long trip into the city.

Betote's friend, Simon, joined him early that morning. Together, they lifted a one-hundred-pound sack of salt onto a small pushcart and quickly began their trek into Douala. The morning air was damp but refreshing. Soon the boys were walking beside the hundreds of palm trees that line the city's streets and streams. Dense un-

Music and dance are important to Betote and Shumba—and to people throughout Cameroon.

dergrowth was everywhere in this low coastal city. Betote began to think about his new business.

It had all started during the last term of school. Betote had been very interested in music, and his teacher had been impressed with Betote's talent. Often Betote had sung for his classmates and at festivals and school events.

It was not long before Betote knew every popular song played on the radio. A few of the older boys in the neighborhood had made their own rhythm instruments and had often played along with the radio.

Betote enjoyed listening to them, but he enjoyed even more listening to Congolese bands that sometimes played in the area. Betote had been very impressed by their modern musical instruments, especially their guitars. Betote's teacher had said that he would teach Betote to play the guitar, but that Betote needed his own instrument.

Betote's father had been unwilling to pay for a guitar. He was not really sure how serious Betote was about his new musical interest. So he had suggested that Betote try to earn the money himself.

In one of his recent trading deals,

Betote's father had acquired a shipment of salt at a very low price. He had agreed to let Betote take four bags of the salt. Since salt is very scarce in interior Cameroon, Betote had decided that he could probably sell a good amount of salt at the train depot.

The marketplace was already crowded when Betote and Simon arrived with their pushcart. They set up a stall next to some other vendors. Betote and Simon arranged their bags very neatly. There they waited. To pass the time, Betote and Simon sang songs. They made up funny words to the music; the words told the boys' story of their wishes to buy a new guitar. Soon crowds of spectators began to listen, and little by little, the salt began to sell.

The day at the market was a long one, and the boys were quite tired when they returned home. Over dinner, the boys told of their first day of business. Betote even sang one of his newly created songs.

Betote's mother sighed. She liked to watch her children enjoy themselves, but she did not understand these loud, new musical sounds. And she still didn't know that Elvis Presley or James Brown were American popular singers, even though her son talked about them all the time.

CAMEROON MINISTRY OF INFORMATION AND TOURISM

Shumba's family lives in an apartment building something like this one.

SHUMBA OF YAOUNDE

Shumba lives in the government apartments near downtown Yaounde, capital of Cameroon. Her father works for the Ministry of Information and Tourism. He has been assigned to the capital for two years. It was quite a change from his previous post at Garoua, in the north.

Fourteen-year-old Shumba attends a large secondary school in the center of Yaounde. She studies English, French, mathematics, literature, biology, geography, and health education. The students must all study very hard to keep their grades high. In order for a student to be eligible for higher education in Cameroon, the student must pass a series of examinations. Shumba did very well in her primary-school examinations. She hopes to continue to do well so she can attend the university someday.

Shumba was excited. Today was Independence Day. For weeks, she and many other children in Cameroon had been practicing for the Independence Day celebration. Shumba and a group from her school were doing a gymnastics routine at the Civic Stadium. Like other children, their costumes were in Cameroon's national colors—green, red, and yellow. Shumba is especially fond of her new scarf, part of her costume. She thinks this multicolored scarf makes her look a little older and prettier. Sometimes in the evening, when her younger brothers are asleep, she tries on her head scarf and admires herself in the mirror.

Though the events at the Civic Stadium did not begin until two in the afternoon,

The marketplace at Yaounde.

Shumba might attend the new and modern University of Cameroon, located in Yaounde.

Shumba and her friends left for the school at ten. They planned to practice their routine a couple of times to make sure they were ready for the main event.

Hundreds of groups were scheduled to participate in the celebrations. Traditional dance groups, choirs, sports, and speeches would all be part of the activities.

Finally, it was time for their routine. Shumba was nervous and her stomach twittered, but somehow she made it through without a single mistake. After the routine, she spotted her family and sat with them. Since her routine was over, she could relax and enjoy the rest of the events.

That night there was a fireworks display. Shumba and her family returned home to watch it. Since their house overlooked the stadium, they had a good view of the event. From their veranda, they watched as reds, yellows, and greens spurted into the sky.

SADOU OF GAROUA

Sadou lives in a compound near the city

23

Sadou sometimes wishes he, too, could learn to read the Koran, the Muslim holy book.

of Garoua, in northern Cameroon. Eleven-year-old Sadou is the third-youngest child in his family. He has four older brothers and sisters. Of the seven children in his family, only the two oldest boys go to school. His older sisters attended primary school for three years. Sadou's parents thought that was enough education for girls. Sadou's father believes that girls are best educated at home, helping their mother with the many household chores.

Sadou and his family are Muslims. The caps worn by the men symbolize them as being members of this religious faith. The clothes that Sadou and his male relatives wear are similar to clothes worn traditionally in Nigeria. The long overgarment comes in a variety of colors and quality. Sadou and his family wear simple cotton-cloth garments for most occasions.

The women wear dresses with gaily colored designs. Their scarves are quite

The cattle Sadou's father raises are probably longhorn cattle, like these. Most of the cattle in Africa are longhorn.

decorative. The women are proud to tie the scarves in the most fashionable styles.

The family compound consists of three structures. The main house is in the center front, with a smaller hut for cooking to its rear. A new building adjoining the main house is under construction. Sadou's father is building this house for the older boys to sleep in. The building has been under construction for several weeks. It requires a lot of time and patience, and Sadou's father is a busy man. He has a large herd of cattle and goats to look after, and assists a few relatives with their local fish market in his spare time.

Sadou is his father's chief "tool-

25

holding" helper. As Sadou's father works on the construction of the new sleeping quarters, it is Sadou's job to hand up new palm poles and batches of elephant grass as needed. While working, Sadou's father talks constantly about the responsibilities of one's home.

Sadou's father tells his son that having a family is a great responsibility. Often Sadou is lectured on the importance of providing a good home and enough food for one's wife and children. Sadou knows that his father is proud of his home and family. But Sadou often daydreams and misses some of what his father says.

In the shade of the compound, Sadou and his friends often play a game called *Oware* with their mankala board. Vari-ations of this game are played in many parts of the world. Sadou is very good at Oware and moves his pebbles swiftly along the board, capturing many of his opponent's pebbles.

Recently, a meat-packing plant was built in Garoua. The plant provided jobs for many men in the production and processing of meat and canned meat products. One day Sadou's friend's father took Sadou through the plant. At first, the strange odors and sounds bothered him. But soon Sadou became accustomed to the smells and sounds and was fascinated by the enormous machines and sounds of this modern, bustling facility. Sadou hopes that when he is older, he can work in a modern factory.

Cameroon Yesterday

Throughout the years, Cameroon has played host to hundreds of ethnic groups who at one time or another called parts of this land "home." In fact, so many peoples have lived in this region over hundreds of years that many people refer to Cameroon as "the racial crossroads of Africa."

EARLY HISTORY

During the Neolithic Age, little movement of peoples occurred throughout Africa. Not until the Iron Age evolved did people find it possible to relocate themselves fairly easily. It is believed that the people of the Cameroon highlands may have learned how to work iron as early as the third century B.C. These highland people may also be the original ancestors of the Bantu-speaking people.

Once they were familiar with the workings of iron, these early people were able to make their own tools and weapons. When iron-bladed axes were created, the people were able to clear land more rapidly. Iron tools for digging and cultivating were also developed, making farming tasks much easier. People became much more independent as a result of the discovery of ironworking.

EARLY BANTU MIGRATION

Some of the Bantu people remained in the highlands to develop their farmlands and expand their village life. Others moved on. There are a number of possible reasons for the Bantu migration. Perhaps these early people wanted more land. With their new iron tools, they could

27

cultivate more land without adding greatly to their workload. Perhaps the population of Bantus increased, forcing the excess people to seek new land. Local feuds or warfare may have occurred, prompting some people to seek safety in other regions. Perhaps a pioneering spirit was aroused in some of the Bantu people. It is possible that some of the more adventuresome wanted to see what the land was like beyond the great forested areas of the Cameroon highlands. No one knows for sure. But whatever the reason for their migration, many Bantu left the highlands to seek homelands elsewhere.

The introduction of several new agricultural crops to the area made the Bantu migration easier. By the fifth century A.D., banana and yam plants were being cultivated in western Africa. These two crops adapted immediately to the hot, moist climate of the equatorial region, and they were also easily transplanted. Thus, it was easy for migrating people to carry these new plants with them, planting and harvesting the crops on their new farmlands.

The migration of Bantus throughout Cameroon took hundreds of years. Normally, the Bantu expansion into new regions was a peaceful event. Pygmies of southern Cameroon probably helped the Bantu acquire meat and other foods during their migrations. But the pygmies were unwilling to give up their own lands to travel with and work for their farming neighbors. The pygmies preferred to retain their ancestral forest homelands and their traditional way of life.

As some Bantu moved beyond Cameroon, other people from the north, west, and east moved into the region. Though none of these ethnic groups had a written language, their history has been passed on orally from generation to generation. The story of the Bafut people passed on this way.

THE BAFUT SETTLEMENT

Hundreds of years ago, the Bafut people were part of the Tikari group of people, who lived in the savanna lands of Nigeria, Chad, and the Sudan. Oppressive slave raiders had forced many Tikari into the North African slave markets. Hoping to avoid such harsh treatment and to find a peaceful life, some Tikaris moved southward.

After establishing a village for themselves near what is now Foumban, Cameroon, they were once again attacked by Fulani slave raiders from the north. After fierce fighting, the people again moved away to seek safety. Eventually, these wanderers settled farther south.

Traditions relate that when the chief died, his three sons quarreled over their father's title. Unable to decide who should be chief, the villagers split into three

Bananas have been grown in Cameroon since at least the fifth century. They are still one of the country's most important crops.

These modern brass figures were cast with the ancient lost-wax method, which has been used by Cameroon's craft workers for centuries.

groups. The chief, or Fon, as he was called, of one group established himself as a strong ruler. He and his people began to construct a new village.

As oral history relates, one day the Fon's mother took a long walk far from the newly developing village. Soon she came upon a lush valley. The Fon's mother thought that this site would be safer and much more valuable as a permanent village. Returning as swiftly as possible, she told her son of the wonderful location nearby. The Fon sent a group of his trusted advisers to see the place.

Everyone was greatly impressed with the new location. Soon the Fon and all his followers moved down from their hills and established a permanent settlement, known today as Bafia. The people have lived in this location for more than three hundred years. Today it is one of the most densely settled areas in equatorial Africa.

EUROPEANS VISIT CAMEROON

During the fifteenth century, the Portuguese began sailing along the west coast of Africa, hoping to find a short route to India. Gradually, their voyages ventured farther and farther along the African coast.

In 1472 Fernao de Po and his sailors sailed to the Gulf of Guinea. They explored an island there, which was later named "Fernando Po." They also sailed into the calm waters of the Wouri River estuary at Douala. The Portuguese seamen called the land *Camaroes,* meaning "prawns" or "crayfish," which were plentiful in the estuary. Douala made an excellent harbor for sailing vessels. Portuguese and other ships later used this estuary as a harbor.

THE SLAVE TRADE

By the middle of the seventeenth century, many settlements in both North and South America had become major markets for slaves. These areas placed heavy

People always fished at Douala's harbor. Here, poles for fish traps lie along the water's edge.

demands on the slave traders for great numbers of slaves. It was not long before the greedy slave merchants sought out the calm harbor of Douala as an ideal loading port for newly acquired West African slaves. The island of Fernando Po was also used as a slave port.

In Douala the local African traders had been dealing with the Europeans for many years. Originally, the Europeans only wanted the Africans' ivory and palm oil, but soon they wanted slaves, too. Sometimes out of fear of being sold into slavery themselves, but more often for the sake of profit, many Douala traders became deeply involved in this business. They worked as middlemen, obtaining slaves by raiding interior villages. People captured in these raids were marched to the coast. At Douala, these unfortunate people were boarded onto ships for eventual sale in the world's slave markets.

The existence of a market for captured slaves encouraged rival tribes to fight each other. Prisoners of these battles were eagerly purchased by the Europeans for the slave trade. Such actions often caused increased hostility between African peoples—a hostility that has, in some cases, lasted into the twentieth century.

THE BRITISH

In the early nineteenth century, the British decided to make the slave trade illegal. Many British warships soon began cruising the west coast of Africa in an attempt to apprehend any illegal slaving vessels. When slave ships were caught, the British patrols freed the captives on board. But the freed slaves and the Europeans did not understand each others' language.

This large home, which once belonged to a European colonialist, is now falling into disrepair.

The woman at left is head of the corn-mill society in Bamendankwe. Many cooperative societies were originally created by Christian missionaries many centuries ago.

Usually the freed people were left in the ports closest to where they were found.

Many missionary groups from Britain came to the ports to help the freed people return home or try to relocate themselves. In 1845 a group of British Baptists formed settlements on the island of Fernando Po and the Cameroon coastland. The island group was led by Alfred Saker and assisted by a group of Christian blacks from Jamaica. They offered medical aid, food, shelter, and sometimes transportation home to the freed slaves.

In 1858 Saker and his followers moved to Cameroon's coastal mainland. Supposedly, Saker convinced a Douala king to sell him a strip of land along the foothills of Mount Cameroon for two thousand British pounds. There, Alfred Saker established a Baptist settlement and called the village Victoria, in honor of the queen of England.

Other British subjects had already settled in this region and continued to arrive after the village of Victoria was established. Some came to farm, while others set up small trading companies. Many of these British subjects hoped that England would eventually take Cameroon as a colony. But at this time, the British government had no official rights or claims to any of this land.

THE IMPACT OF ISLAM

Meanwhile, in Cameroon's northern interior, the impact of changes in neighboring Nigeria were being felt. A series of well-organized states in northern Nigeria had been captured in the early nineteenth century by the Muslim soldier Utuman Dan Fodio and his Fulani cavalry. They then extended their raids into the western Cameroon kingdoms of the Bamun peoples. The Bamun were defeated and their city sacked by the superior Fulani cavalry. Only by digging great trenches around their towns were the Bamun able to defeat later Fulani attacks.

In far northern Cameroon, the religion of Islam had already spread among the people. But among the Bamun, it did not become popular until the 1880s. However, large parts of the western highlands did come under the control of the Fulani sultan of Adamawa. Here Islamic religion and culture took hold.

TRADE AGREEMENTS AND TREATIES

During this period, Britain had reached several trade agreements with the Douala people. The British were interested in Cameroon's ivory and palm oil. Under the arrangements, Britain had no expense of operating a colonial government, yet it was able to share Cameroon's raw materials cheaply.

Eventually, though, enough concern for the region developed, and Britain decided that it would acquire Cameroon as a colony. The British Parliament decided to send Edward Hewett to conclude treaties with the Douala chiefs, thus ensuring the area as a colony for Britain.

Immediately, Hewett sailed for West Africa. Arriving at the port of Douala on July 13, 1884, he discovered that representatives of the German government had signed treaties with two Douala kings six days before! Thereafter, he was known as "Too Late Hewett."

GERMAN RULE

According to the treaties that Gustav

Traditional Muslim rulers are still very powerful in northern Cameroon. Here, the man who was Emir of Dikwa in the 1950s is shown in his ceremonial costume.

German settlers operated huge cacao plantations in colonial Cameroon and cacao is still one of Cameroon's most important export crops. This worker is spreading the cacao nibs on a straw mat for drying (above). Later (opposite), he examines some of the nibs to see if they have dried.

Nachtigal of Germany signed that day, the Douala people would forever retain their rights as sole traders in the area. This enabled the Douala tradesmen to continue their monopoly on trade with no interference from the new German colonizers.

At first, the Germans were interested only in the rich farmlands of the foothills of Mount Cameroon, which they hoped to turn into plantations. The German settlers hoped that large banana, cacao, oil palm, and rubber plantations would reap rich profits. But they had no intention of paying high wages for African labor. The Douala, however, had no desire to work for the German plantation owners; they had their own trading businesses.

Some adventuresome German traders made exploratory trips into the interior of the colony. They discovered that the people of the interior were willing to trade directly with them. Thus, the Germans

36

eliminated the middlemen, the Douala, and increased their personal profits. But this angered Douala traders, since the German treaties had guaranteed them exclusive rights to trade with the interior. The German colonizers were breaking the agreements of the treaties.

As the German traders developed their trade in the interior, they discovered a need for great numbers of African laborers. Once goods were purchased in the interior, the goods had to be carried to the coast. Many workers were needed for this job. But few people were willing to leave their villages for long periods of time. They also resented the Germans for offering low pay for this hard task. Thus,

the traders had a hard time getting the labor forces they needed.

As the plantations and trading companies grew, they were competing for cheap African laborers. The farms were soon successfully producing quantities of bananas, cacao, and palm kernels. In order to maintain a high level of production, the farmers sent recruiting agents to the interior to bring back African laborers. The trading companies began to do the same thing.

African laborers usually had to sign a two-year contract to work on one of the coastal plantations. Housing conditions for the laborers were substandard and food was meager and of poor quality. Soon

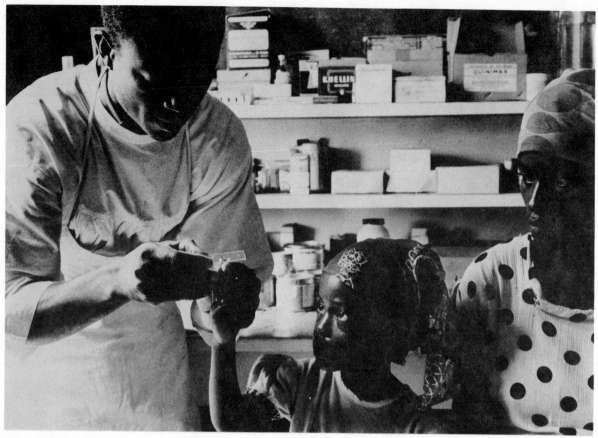

Work goes on to eradicate the dread tropical disease malaria. Above: A medical assistant takes a blood sample to test for the disease. Opposite top: Food is removed before an area is sprayed against the Anopheles mosquito, which carries malaria. Opposite bottom: Workers are spraying a hut.

malnutrition and disease among African laborers became a major problem. Having lived in the hills, these African people were unaccustomed to malaria and black-water fever. Their bodies had not developed any immunities against these diseases. When they came to the coast, hundreds of Africans died from these diseases.

Some Africans preferred to work for the traders rather than the plantation owners.

At least with the trader's job, a person could leave after making a round trip to the coast. There was no two-year contract to force one into long periods of labor service. Thus, many men, women, and children were carrying heavy loads of products from the interior to the coast.

Soon the overseers' bad treatment of African laborers became well known to other Africans. When recruiting agents of

either the traders or the plantation owners came into a village to recruit laborers, it was rarely a happy time. Some villagers considered the recruiting officers as "agents of death." Sometimes the agents were resisted or even killed by angry villagers when they entered the interior.

But German traders and plantation owners were unwilling to give up easily their quest for cheap labor. The Germans encouraged the colonial government to impose heavy taxes on the Africans for government services. Local Africans who were unable to pay these taxes in cash were usually forced into labor camps on the plantations or forced onto trading routes in order to pay off their tax debt.

Despite the protests of the African people, thousands were forced into such labor. About half the people recruited from the interior during these years never returned home again. Although some of these people relocated themselves in coastal villages, an extremely high death rate took its toll on African lives.

THE KING PROTESTS

By 1914 the Douala people of the coast had become extremely angry with the German colonizers. Besides taking their trading-rights monopoly away, the Germans were trying to move the Douala people off their coastal property.

King Manga Bell and his Douala people sent a representative to Germany to plead their case. If the German government refused them, the King planned to ask the French or British for help.

But stirrings of World War I were in the air. The Germans considered the French and British their enemies. Colonial officials in Cameroon considered King Manga's actions as treason. King Manga Bell was soon arrested and hanged for his act of protest. His resistance was to inspire later nationalist leaders.

END OF GERMAN RULE

Just before the war, the Germans began to invest in and develop their colony, which they called Kamerun.

During World War I, both French and British colonial forces occupied the German colony. Following the war in 1919, the League of Nations ruled that Germany must surrender its rights to Kamerun. The League claimed that Germany had mismanaged the colony and was incapable of running a colonial government. But, in fact, German colonialism was no worse than French or British.

The League awarded part of the colony to France and part to Britain. France received the largest portion, as much of Kamerun bordered France's other central African colonies. England received the remaining portion, which adjoined England's Nigerian colony. The spelling of the colony's name, Kamerun, changed slightly with new translations. The French colony was called Cameroun and the British section was called Cameroon.

This division of the country was resented by some Cameroonian leaders. Different colonial languages and cultures made the task of reunification more difficult in later years.

CAMEROON AND CAMEROUN

During their colonial rule of Cameroun, the French completed the railway line that was being built from Douala on the coast to Yaounde in the highlands. They also moved the colonial headquarters from the Mount Cameroon hillside to Yaounde. With the railway completed into the highlands, the French thought the new capital might encourage greater opportunities for colonial development and trade. French colonialists also preferred Yaounde's climate. Neither the French nor the British, however, made any great attempt during these years to encourage the development of the economy for the African people.

In 1940, when World War II began, the French colonial government in Cameroun refused to recognize the Vichy (Nazi-controlled) government of German-occupied France. Thus, Cameroun was maintained as a part of "Free France" (French-controlled France), and the colony was used as a training ground for some Free French troops. Later many of them helped liberate North Africa.

At the end of the war, the United Nations was created to replace the League of Nations. The UN established the Cameroon-Cameroun areas as British and French trusteeships. This meant that the European governments were to assist the local people in forming their own system of government, with majority rule. Thus a period of progress began, geared toward the development of self-government for these territories. Independence was now guaranteed for these lands.

Cameroon Today

THE PEOPLE DEMAND SELF-GOVERNMENT

After World War II, many African leaders worked hard to achieve independence for their native lands. The desire for self-government was very strong in much of West Africa.

Each territory seemed to have its own unique problems, and the territories of French Cameroun and British Cameroon were no exception. No other African territory had been ruled by three colonial powers plus two international governing bodies. The division of the territory between France and England had created a number of problems for the African people who lived there.

After the war, some African nationalist groups began to pressure France and England to free the territories. The greatest pressure was felt within the French territory, where radical militants in the south demanded an immediate end to French rule. Rebel fighting broke out in parts of Cameroun. In 1955 the "Bamileke Rebellion" took place against both the French colonial authorities and the northern party (led by Ahmadou Ahidjo), which was regarded as too moderate.

Outbreaks of riots and violence over the next three years cost the lives of thousands of Africans and the destruction of many public buildings. Finally, the French captured many of the rebel fighters, banishing suspected rebel leaders from the territory.

Ancient, primitive ways of life are still found in isolated villages throughout Cameroon.

CAMEROON MINISTRY OF INFORMATION AND TOURISM

43

Local chiefs and elders meet with a United Nations group that toured British Cameroon in 1958.

Other rebel leaders eventually came to terms with Ahidjo's provisional government, which offered amnesty to its former opponents.

Meanwhile, some groups in Cameroun insisted on unification with British Cameroon. But not all governmental leaders believed that the people of both territories wanted unification. The UN was anxious to see the former "trust," or "mandate," territories free, but it wanted the local people to make the choice for independence and/or unification.

The first formal step toward independence occurred in 1958, when the UN General Assembly voted to end the French trusteeship in Cameroun. On January 1, 1960, Cameroun gained its independence—the second French-speaking territory to do so. The nation was called the United Republic of Cameroon, and its new leader was Ahmadou Ahidjo.

PROBLEMS OF UNIFICATION

Many citizens of the newly independent Cameroon wanted to unite with the colony of British Cameroons. President Ahidjo faced one of the nation's most critical problems.

British Cameroons actually consisted of two separate regions of land, both of which shared a common border with Nigeria. These regions were called North Cameroon and South Cameroon. Under the existing British colonial policy, these regions were governed through the colonial offices in Nigeria. Although some of the people in these territories shared similarities in language and culture with neighboring Nigerians, most of the people did not. With the question of unification on everyone's mind, turmoil and dispute raged throughout the land.

Some people in these British territories wanted to be joined with Nigeria, while others wanted to unite with independent Cameroon. Still others wanted to remain a British colony and not unite with either Cameroon or Nigeria. The entire question of unification between the Cameroons became an emotional political issue. At times, fighting and riots erupted between

The territorial assembly of French Cameroun in session in the 1950s.

UNITED NATIONS

El Hadj Ahmadou Ahidjo, president of Cameroon, at ceremonies in Garoua, 1969.

people with different opinions regarding unification.

The United Nations finally stepped in to help settle the question. The UN insisted that the people of North and South Cameroon decide their own fate. An election was held in February of 1961, in which the people were told to choose between joining independent Cameroon or Nigeria. The results of the election caused even more conflict. The people in the northern territory voted to join with Nigeria, while those in the southern region voted to join with Cameroon.

Immediately, a storm of protest was raised over the election procedures. Some people claimed that the election results had not been properly tabulated. Others charged that the UN had not interpreted the results properly.

Such international unhappiness was aroused over the vote that the entire issue was brought before the World Court. This international body of justice ruled on June 1, 1961, that the election returns were valid and a true reflection of the desires of the people of North and South Cameroon. Therefore, the northern region was joined to Nigeria and the southern portion united with Cameroon on October 1, 1961.

EL HADJ AHMADOU AHIDJO

Ahidjo was born in northern Cameroon in 1924. After graduating from college in Yaounde, he worked in a variety of civil service jobs for the colonial government.

In 1947 Ahidjo was elected to the first Cameroon Representative Assembly. From then on, he spent all his time working for independence for the colony. Eventually, he even formed his own political party. Having worked so hard for the nation's freedom, it was no surprise when he was elected first president of the new nation.

Not only had Ahidjo gained the respect and admiration of his own people, but

CAMEROON

REGIONS

NORTHERN

WEST CAMEROON

WESTERN

SOUTH

COASTAL

CENTRAL

EASTERN

other African leaders respected and admired him as well. His leadership abilities were recognized by the members of the Organization of African Unity (OAU) when he was elected the OAU's president in 1969. Ahidjo has earned international recognition through the several honorary doctorate degrees that American and French universities have presented him.

A TWO-STATE NATION IS FORMED

Now that the question of unification was settled, President Ahidjo and his government had to recreate their government structure to provide for the additional territory. It was decided that two federal states would be created for governing purposes. What had once been French Cameroun would be referred to as East Cameroon. The newly acquired territory of South Cameroon would be called West Cameroon.

President Ahidjo was from East Cameroon. It was agreed that the prime minister of West Cameroon would be the nation's vice-president. Thus, the constitution of the United Republic of Cameroon states that the president and vice-president be from different states. The two states were further divided into six administrative regions, which in turn were divided into departments and districts.

During the push for independence, many political parties were active in the fight for freedom and unification. In East Cameroon in 1961, the Cameroonian Union Party, headed by Ahmadou Ahidjo, received majority support. In the west, John N. Foncha's Kamerun National Democratic Party was in control. In 1962 these two parties joined together to form one strong parliamentary group, which supported national unity.

President Ahidjo appealed to the leaders of the diverse political parties still active within the nation to join together for the mutual welfare of the new nation. Like other leaders in Africa, President Ahidjo believed that the basic objectives of the nation's political parties were more alike than different.

Eventually, a one-party political system evolved in Cameroon, called the National Cameroon Union. It is the belief of the nation's leaders that greater efforts can be made to strengthen the economic and social welfare of the country through the united efforts of all the leaders in a one-party political system.

Ahidjo's government has strengthened the power of the central (federal) government over the regions and the role of the chief executive. Over the years, President Ahidjo has also become stronger in terms of personal rule.

THE GOVERNMENT

The new constitution created the Federal Republic of Cameroon. The constitution provided for executive, legislative, and judicial divisions in the govern-

A Kanuri woman with her sons.

ment. It also allowed for a degree of autonomy between the two states—East and West Cameroon. In the popular elections of May 20, 1972, the nation was officially renamed the United Republic of Cameroon.

The executive branch of the government includes the offices of president and vice-president. Both president and vice-president are elected by the people during secret balloting for five-year terms. The president is allowed to select members of his Cabinet, as well as the prime ministers of the two states. The president is the official head of the military; he has the power to issue emergency decrees should situations warrant them. Although the vice-president has no special duties, he is expected to assist the president in the execution of the duties of that office.

The legislative power of the nation is held by the National Federal Assembly.

Delegates to the Assembly are also elected by secret ballot. Representation for the Assembly is based on the population. For every eighty thousand people in a district, one representative is selected. Since no official census had been taken in Cameroon, the population was estimated. Forty Assembly positions were created for East Cameroon and ten for West Cameroon.

The National Federal Assembly deals with the country's budget and the government's legal workings. Approved acts of legislation are forwarded from the Assembly to the president for approval.

The judicial branch of the federal government has two major court systems. The Federal Court of Justice is the final court of appeals for cases that arise out of either state court. Cameroon also has a High Court of Justice. This special court was established to try cases of high treason or conspiracy against the government or to judge misconduct of government officials.

Each of the nation's two states—East and West Cameroon—have an appointed prime minister and an elected state legislative assembly. The state assemblies are responsible for those powers not specifically granted to the National Assembly.

INDEPENDENCE DAY

Like many new nations, Independence Day is an important time for celebration in the United Republic of Cameroon. Usually the national flag and national colors are prominently displayed on all government buildings, schools, commercial buildings, and homes.

The national colors are green, red, and yellow. The flag is a tricolor of three vertical stripes. The far-left stripe is green, symbolizing the rich vegetation of the southern region. The red stripe in the center represents the supreme power of the national government. The yellow stripe on the right stands for the bright sunshine of northern Cameroon. In the green stripe are two gold stars, which represent the country's two states—East and West Cameroon.

On Independence Day, there are usually parades in the center of towns. The parades bring together the local people. Often local government officials read a speech from the president, prepared for this important holiday. Marching bands, civic groups, school groups, and athletic organizations often join together in the parade. Later in the day, the groups participate in singing festivals, dancing, and athletic competitions. The nation's national anthem, "O Cameroon, Land of our Ancestors," is always sung.

EDUCATION

One major effect of the unification of East and West Cameroon was that the nation had to deal with new problems in education. In West Cameroon, the school system was modeled after the British system, with English as the language of instruction. In East Cameroon, the educa-

Citizens attend a political rally at Sangmelima in 1964.

tional system had been patterned after the French, with classes taught in French. Children in each state studied different subjects and had different school-year calendars. Textbooks and teaching methods varied widely between the two areas. Opportunities for higher education differed as well.

The government decided to handle the language problem first. Since Cameroon had established itself as a bilingual country, it was decided that schooling should be bilingual as well. Therefore, in the West, where English was normally used, French would be a required subject in all grades beyond the primary level. In the

East, where French was normally used, English would be required. It was hoped that this would ease the language situation.

The state governments were asked to coordinate their school systems so their holidays fell on the same days and their school years were the same length. The state governments were also asked to plan a basic education program that was the same for all students in both states.

As is true of many African and European school systems, a primary-school graduate in Cameroon is required to pass an exam in order to continue to secondary school. Sometimes students who do not qualify for entrance into secondary school may enter a vocational institute instead. There they could study teacher training, homemaking, agricultural education, and some artisan skills. Most of these schools are located in East Cameroon, but more are being built in West Cameroon to provide equal opportunities to the youth of that state. Cameroon has one of the highest public school enrollments among African nations.

Critics of the Cameroon educational

These children are starting to learn how to write.

The school these children attend is so overcrowded that their class must be held on the porch.

system point out the high dropout rate for secondary-school students. Out of every ten students starting primary school in 1968, only four completed the sixth grade. Cameroon's educational leaders, concerned about these figures, have been trying to improve all aspects of the educational system.

Cameroon is proud of its university at Yaounde, where students can pursue degrees in law, science, and liberal arts. Recently, there have been moves to "Africanize" both the staff and the subject matter of the university.

The Center for African Research at Yaounde also provides additional higher-educational opportunities for many students. This center attracts many of Africa's top scholars. Plans for a medical school there are presently under way.

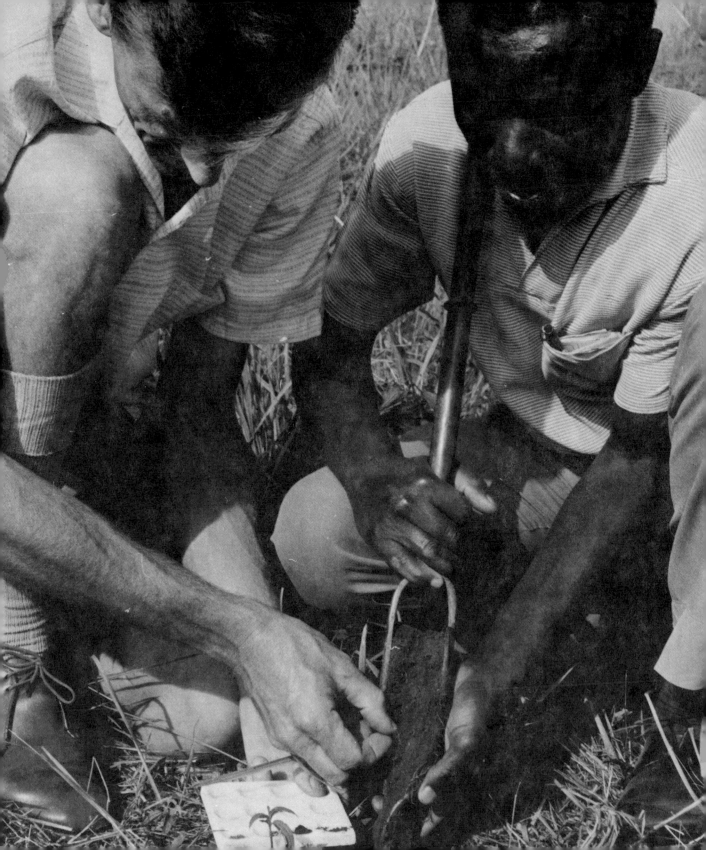

Natural Treasures

The land of Cameroon is host to a variety of living plants and animals. Some of these have been recognized by the local people for their unique value.

Many of the animals have been included in traditional customs. The leopard, for example, is considered the wisest and strongest of all animals, according to the Banyang people of West Cameroon. Therefore, if any Banyang kills a leopard, the hunter is supposed to present the animal to the village chief. The kill is then shared with all of the villagers. It is believed that the hunter must possess great wisdom and strength in order to have killed the leopard. The sharing of the kill thus demonstrates the hunter's respect for the village leaders and his willingness to share his talents with other villagers.

In some villages, animals are rated for their importance to the animal community. In addition to the leopard, the python, the crocodile, and the elephant are also important animals that are greatly respected by the people of Cameroon. Common animals with less traditional importance include the antelope, bushpig, anteater, and baboon. As is the custom with the leopard kill, certain social obligations are expected of any hunter who kills one of the respected members of the animal community. The custom varies according to the degree of the animal's importance.

THE PYTHON

This snake commands a high position of

United Nations soil-survey experts take a sample of Cameroon's soil.

Elephants large and small roam in their natural surroundings at the Waza Game Reserve.

respect in Cameroon's animal community. The python is often found in the country's hot, tropical regions. It thrives near the marshes and rivers of the coastal and southern lowland areas.

A mature python is usually between fourteen and eighteen feet long; a record length of thirty feet was once reported. The python has a very attractive skin, its color varying from a yellowish-brown to gray, with a chainlike design or pattern in darker brown or black.

The python is a constrictor snake, which means that it will coil around its victim and crush it to death. Then the snake will swallow the carcass whole. Its jawbones detach, allowing it to swallow large-sized animals. Once the carcass has been swallowed, the digestive juices in the snake's stomach begin to break down the victim's tissues.

Pythons have been observed hanging

head down from high trees. In this position, the snake is almost motionless. Supposedly, the snake hangs this way so it can fall rapidly onto an unsuspecting victim walking below.

There are many folktales and legends concerning the python. Some cultures highly respect the python and praise its presence. Some folktales attribute almost supernatural powers to this snake.

One popular story is that the python can assume the vocal power of its intended victim. For instance, if a dog would happen to stray near the marshes where the python was hanging, the snake would be able to bark like the dog. The barking would supposedly lure the curious dog closer into the marshes until the animal was close to the snake. The python would then catch the dog. Children are often told not to venture into strange places if they hear their names called by an unfamiliar voice, since it could be the python lying in wait!

Herdsmen from Sangmelima bring their cattle from the Niger River to Cameroon's capital, Yaounde.

AIR AFRIQUE

Proud and graceful gazelles are native to Cameroon.

ARMY ANTS

Another very unusual inhabitant of Cameroon is the army ant or driver ant. This insect is the central character of many frightening stories. Although parts of the stories about the army ant are true, there is no real justification in their frightening fame.

Army ants on the march will try to eat everything in their path. An awesome sight, these ants form a gigantic mass by swarming around the queen. Vast tentacle-like avenues of worker ants stream out from the mass in all directions seeking food. The food is sent back to satisfy the millions of ants in the center of the colony. While moving, these ants can advance at the rate of sixty-five feet an hour, gathering and killing almost all insects and anything else too sluggish to get out of the way of the advancing army of ants.

Some stories tell of the army ants marching directly through homes that were in their way. Supposedly, people place the legs of their bedposts in pails of vinegar to keep the ants from climbing up and crawling over the people while sleeping. When people see the ants coming, they heap ashes across their doorways. The ants are turned aside.

As a whole, the moving ant colony is comparable to an animal weighing about forty-five pounds and possessing more than twenty thousand mouths and stingers! As a result of such comparisons, the army ant colony is often considered an awesome monster.

WHAT WILL REMAIN?

Along some of the lowland and coastal

This lion cub was caught in a forest. He will stay in Cameroon until he is grown, then will be sent to a zoo in Europe or America.

CAMEROON MINISTRY OF INFORMATION AND TOURISM

areas of Cameroon exist dense groves of mangrove swamps. The tropical forests of this region contain some of the most valuable stands of wood in the world. Huge ebony and mahogany trees rise out of the humid undergrowth of these equatorial forests.

Monkeys, gorillas, and countless species of birds have also made their home in these cathedrals of nature. So, too, have the flies and mosquitoes that have tormented humans and beasts for countless years. Regardless, these living things have existed in harmony with one another in Cameroon for centuries.

The tsetse fly carries the dreaded sleeping sickness, which is often fatal to animals or humans. The tsetse fly has long been an enemy to everything in this part of Africa. It will not be long, however, before this insect is controlled.

The rich grasslands of Cameroon once contained herds of wild animals. Elephants, leopards, antelope, zebras, and giraffes once roamed without interference in this lush landscape. As the human population and colonial settlements increased, however, many of the wildlife species were forced off their lands or killed in excessive quantities. With the growth of urban development, survival for the remaining animals is even more of a problem.

The People Live in Cameroon

THE AFRICAN MELTING POT

Cameroon was the homeland of countless ethnic groups in the past. Although some of the cultural differences remained over the years, living under a common government has brought the people together. Different ethnic groups mixed together and intermarried, and a "melting pot" population evolved. The ethnic characteristics that survived make Cameroon's customs and traditions some of the most interesting in all of Africa.

THE DOUALA OF THE COAST

The Douala were once the largest single group occupying land along Cameroon's coast. Their well-established kingdoms governed the people by a respected system of laws and customs. Their religion was a form of animism, which governed all aspects of their daily lives. During festivals and other religious acts of worship, the people used elaborate facial masks and wooden carvings to aid them in asking blessings or help from their gods. Sometimes the masks were used to represent different forces of nature, which were important to the success of a new crop or harvest. In many ceremonies, music and dance were also used to act out the people's requests or give thanks to an ancestor or a god. The people asked for blessings for newlywed couples, for newborn infants, for recently deceased community members and at other events considered significant to the people.

Although many Douala people still practice forms of traditional animism, early missionary groups converted many

Douala people to the Christian religion.

The coastal Douala were the first people to encounter the Europeans. Folk history relates that the Douala called the Europeans the "toeless people." This was because the Europeans wore shoes and their feet could not be seen.

Most Douala still live along Cameroon's coast. The country's major city, Douala (named after these people), is situated on the southeastern shore of the Wouri River estuary. Many Douala people still consider this city their home. Today, however, the Douala people are no longer the largest ethnic group living in this area.

With the rapid development of harbor trade and other commercial establishments of this large, urban city, there grew a demand for skilled and unskilled workers that could not be met by the local Douala population. Thus, people of many different ethnic groups migrated to the city, hoping to find new and better jobs.

Today the Douala speak a number of languages. As a result of European occupation, some have learned a bit of German, French, and English. Other African languages have also become a part of the people's vocabulary as the Douala dealt with other Africans in their trades. Over the years, the Douala have incorporated some of the influences of other ethnic groups. Today's Douala are quite different than the people the Portuguese sailors first encountered.

THE FANG OF SOUTH-CENTRAL CAMEROON

Around 1800 large groups of Fang people moved southward, settling in the forested regions of south-central Cameroon. There they began to farm. The Fang still live in this area.

According to oral history, the Fang developed a very effective system of communication. Because the farms were large, workers were often far from their village. When someone became suddenly ill or a fire got out of control or an unexpected visitor came to the compound, it was important that messages be sent to the distant workers. In early days, runners relayed the messages in person. But this system was not reliable, so the Fang devised a tonal drum for sending messages. The drums were constructed to enable the production of two tones, a high-pitched and a low-pitched sound. The combination of these tones and a variety of rhythms produced "words"; thus, they created "talking drums."

Another early discovery of the Fang people was the effectiveness of poison as a hunting tool. Since the task of killing large, wild animals was always a very dangerous job for the hunter, centuries ago the Fang perfected an easy way to accomplish this act. They used roots, herbs, and seeds for making a variety of poisons. The hunters' spears and arrows were then

Cameroon's many civilizations and ethnic groups have all left their individual imprint on the country's culture.

dipped into the poisonous solutions. A single hunter could wound an animal from a safe distance. The hunter would watch as the poison reacted on the animal, killing him. This method was safer than using crude, primitive implements, and it required only a few hunters. The animal's death was much quicker this way.

The Fang also had highly advanced knowledge of making medicines from herbs, weeds, and seeds. The Fang not only used their remedies to overcome illnesses, but in later years they shared their medical knowledge with the Europeans who came to their land.

MARRIAGE

Among the Fang, as was true of most other African groups, polygamy (having more than one wife) was a common practice. Polygamy was initiated to insure the survival of the people. In early days, hunters were often killed, leaving young widows. There were always more women in a settlement than men. So more than one woman would join with a man, and each woman could bear children.

With the development of better hunting tools, hunting became safer and fewer hunters were killed. Polygamy became less common. Then a man who had more than one wife commanded special respect. First, he had to be wealthy enough to pay bridewealth (or a dowry) to the family of each woman he married. The man had to be wealthy to take care of his wives and their children. Usually, this man was considered a person of achievement, intelligence, and leadership. The Fang believed that these qualities were necessary for a polygamous man in order for him to keep all his wives and children happy.

The life of a hunter, trader, or farmer was not easy. The women's daily routine was just as strenuous as the men's. The women had to haul water for the daily chores, prepare the food, tend the crops, and care for the children. In a system where polygamy was practiced, as in the Fang society, all the wives shared the chores. Older children assisted, too. Thus, each wife's burden was lightened.

When daughters of a family were married, their husbands had to pay the bride's family bridewealth. The bridewealth was the family's compensation for the loss of their daughter. The bride would move into her husband's family compound and share the work of that family.

The sons had just the opposite responsibility. They had to save enough money to accumulate bridewealth for a wife. When a young man married, however, his family gained the services of the new wife.

Polygamy was a common practice until European missionaries came to Africa. Christian missionaries, with their different life-styles and religious beliefs, frowned on this practice. Often, they forbade their followers to practice polygamy. Many Africans did not understand this strange moral judgment that the missionaries placed on their way of life.

Today many Africans have ceased the

A wedding party on the road between Sangmelima and Yaounde. Wedding parties frequently dance on the highway, blocking traffic, and anyone who wishes to pass must present a gift to the bride.

practice of polygamy. Possibly, the period of colonialism brought about an end to this custom. The system also may have died out because the economic structure of modern Africa no longer requires it. Young Africans still face conflict as they try to adhere to the traditional ways of their elders, yet are influenced by the changing times of an independent nation. But the resulting generation gap is still a problem for the people of Cameroon.

THE BAMUM OF FOUMBAN

In the central highlands live the Bamum

65

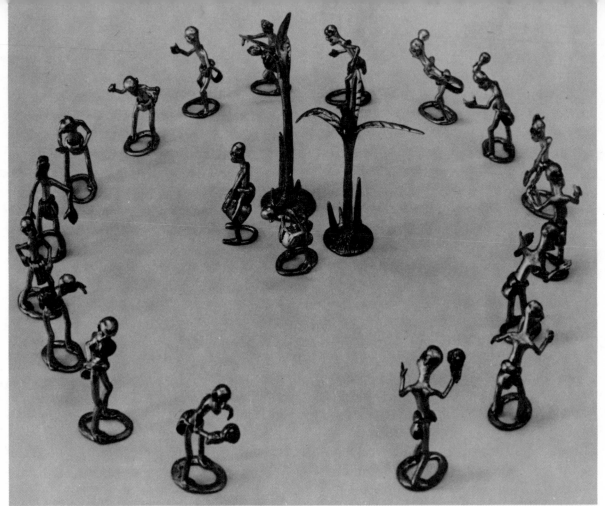

Umaru Njasi, a Bamum, has made a series of brass figurines using the ancient lost-wax casting method. The figurines show daily activities among traditional Cameroonian peoples. Above: This group represents a circle dance of the Suah festival, which is held to assure fertility.

people, who believe they are related historically to the Tikari and Bamileke people. Through the years, the Bamum have retained a very strong sense of cultural identity and are quite proud of their developments. At the end of the nineteenth century, they were converted to Islam. For many years, they have lived peacefully with no outside interference.

The Bamum are ruled by a sultan, or king. (Their leaders have been called by both titles.) One of their noted rulers was King Njoya, who held power at the turn of the twentieth century. Although he was for a time receptive to Christian missionaries, King Njoya was also anxious to have his people retain pride in their traditional ways of life. He was afraid that Westerni-

The materials used in the lost-wax method of casting brass. Top row from left: beeswax for modeling; clay that encloses the model; brass rod; broken brass rod that will be melted. Bottom row from left: new clay mold with two wax models; clay mold after the wax has been "lost" through heating; mold with brass fragments enclosed; mold after brass was melted and flowed into spaces left by "lost" wax; partly opened finished mold.

zation might destroy the customs and culture. Therefore, he tried to encourage his people in their creative arts.

The Bamum made artistic workings in bronze, clay, wood, and other related media. To encourage his people to continue these art forms, King Njoya established a museum at Foumban for the preservation of local mementos and past trophies. He also placed some outstanding contemporary art objects in this museum. Many artisans also earned their living selling some of their pieces to interested African and European art collectors. The people of Bamum origin are proud that King Njoya saved many of their outstanding works of art.

THE BAMILEKE

The largest single ethnic group in the country is the Bamileke, with more than eight hundred thousand people. The Bamileke are broken down into ninety small chiefdoms, speaking many dialects of their basic language. Because of this division, the Bamileke are less unified than other ethnic groups in Cameroon.

Most Bamileke live in Cameroon's central highlands. Traditionally, they were farmers and herders. In recent times, however, several factors have forced these people to leave their ancestral homes.

According to tradition, family land is passed down to the father's eldest son or

A class at one of Cameroon's teacher-training colleges works at basketry, mat making, knotting, and carving in order to maintain and improve native crafts in rural schools.

one son whom he may choose. Other sons and daughters traditionally receive no land; thus, they have had to move out to seek land for themselves. With the country's increasing population, most of the fertile land of the highlands has already been taken. Thus, the younger generation is forced to move farther and farther away from their families in order tó acquire land.

Many young Bamileke men and women have become active in Cameroon's new nationalism. Many of these people have left their homes to seek roles in government or business. The capital city, Yaounde, bustles with eager young Bamileke who seek civil service employment. Others have migrated to the coastal city of Douala in search of work with business firms. So many Bamileke have migrated to Douala that there are presently more Bamileke in that city than the native Douala people.

OTHER GROUPS

In the extreme northern part of the country are some Hausa people. Once the Hausa dominated this area and the land to the north. They were great long-distance traders. Their language was the *lingua franca,* or "common language," of parts of West Africa. Today, however, most Hausa live in neighboring Nigeria, Chad, and Sudan.

In Cameroon's densely forested southern interior some pygmy groups remain. Influenced little by colonialism or independence, the pygmies live much the same way as they did centuries ago. Their struggle is one of subsistence. They ask little of the government and prefer to be left alone.

Few Europeans live in Cameroon; only twenty thousand of the country's 5.7 million people are Europeans. They are German, French, British, or Greek, whose ancestors came to the area during the colonial period. Although some Europeans

Two Fulani girls of northern Cameroon.

are still engaged in plantation farming, most have settled in the cities of Douala and Yaounde.

AFRICA'S LOST TREASURES

Some people say that traditional art in Africa is a phenomenon of the past. Since much of the art was related to the people's animist religion, Islam and Christianity had negative effects on traditional art. As missionaries encouraged the Africans to accept a new religion, they simultaneously discouraged African artists from creating the masks, sculpture, dances, and songs that were a part of their traditional religion. Thus, as Christianity and Islam increased, less and less traditional art was created.

Strangely, though, while many Europeans were discouraging Africans from their daily religious practices and rituals, the traditional art works were being collected by other Europeans. The works were sold to museums and private collectors

Residents of Sangmelima help a neighbor build a new home.

throughout the world. Today these religious treasures can be seen in many European and American art museums.

Cameroon is trying to collect and preserve its remaining art objects. The government would also like to regain much of the art that was taken out of the country. Contemporary Cameroonian artists are receiving government support.

Cultural exchange programs have recently been introduced in Cameroon's urban areas. Most of the programs are the result of French interest in the country. French literature, art, music, and drama are being introduced at the centers. The government hopes that the people of Cameroon will soon be able to share their art forms with France and other nations.

SOCIAL AND RACIAL PROBLEMS

In the United Republic of Cameroon, the spirit of nationalism is a relatively new phenomenon. Prior to independence, the many peoples of Cameroon had never been united. The people were united within their own groups, with a common ancestral background, language, and religion. Under its own leader, each group—whether a large kingdom or a small village—established its own laws and system of justice. Thus, deep traditions and traditional loyalties were the major force in the people's daily lives.

National unity is a hard concept for the people—especially the older ones—to grasp. They are proud of their independence and their ethnic group. Never before have they had a reason to unite with other groups. But as older people struggle to retain their traditional, independent ways, young people are attracted by the ideas of Westernization and national unity, and by modern technology.

Problems have developed between various ethnic groups. Some, especially the Douala, resent the great Bamileke migration into "their city." Others resent the high proportion of Bamileke who work in government and public service. Others feel that the Bamileke have too much control in the government and that they are favored by government officials. Yet the Bamileke are the largest population group in the country. Thus, it is not surprising that many Bamileke serve as government officials.

UNITED NATIONS

Patients at a clinic at Banda are being examined by local and United Nations physicians, medical assistants, and nurses.

TRADE UNIONS

Trade unions in both East and West Cameroon have proved very important for the local people. The unions have not only acted as spokesmen for the workers' welfare and interest, but many unions

These students at the Federal Superior School of Agriculture are learning entomology (the study of insects) in preparation for employment by government agricultural services.

have also acted as a type of social club for new workers in the cities.

It is not always easy for a rural villager to adjust to the ways of the city. The problems of adapting to paying cash for things are often difficult for someone used to trading and bargaining goods for goods. The trade unions help people locate people in the city and find adequate housing. They also aid their members in case of an emergency, such as loss of job, sudden burial expenses, unexpected medical bills. Some unions also provide education and guidance to younger people who seek jobs.

HEALTH

Cameroon has long been plagued by a

number of endemic (native) tropical diseases, including malaria, yellow fever, blackwater fever, dysentery, pneumonia, and sleeping sickness. These diseases have disabled and killed countless people over the centuries.

Leprosy is one of the most dreaded diseases in Cameroon. At present, there are approximately thirty hospitals and leper villages in Cameroon that provide aid and services to infected and disabled leper victims. These are both public and private facilities. Research is being conducted to find new ways of treating and preventing this dreaded disease.

Malnutrition and a high rate of infant mortality still pose serious problems for Cameroon. Through health-education programs set up by the government, proper diet and prenatal care can assist in preventing or at least diminishing these problems. The government has allocated a high proportion of its budget to building new medical dispensaries, hospitals, and health information centers. Although many more doctors are needed in Cameroon, midwives, nurses, and nursing assistants have greatly helped serve in the new urban and rural clinics. Missionaries also assist in the country's medical services. Teams of "Flying Doctors" recruited from missionary groups can bring health services to many remote regions of the country.

The People Work in Cameroon

IMPORTANT AGRICULTURAL PRODUCTS

For centuries, most of the people of Cameroon grew their own food. Currently more than 80 percent of the nation's labor force is involved in agriculture. Cash-crop production (crops sold by the growers) accounts for about 80 percent of the nation's revenues.

Cacao is one of Cameroon's leading cash crops. The seeds of the cacao tree are used to make cocoa and chocolate. Many cacao plantations were originally established during the German colonial period. Long since turned over to Cameroonian control and production, these plantations have continued to be valuable.

It is believed that the cacao tree was imported from Central or South America. Once established in West Africa, this tree flourished. Cameroon's warm, moist lowlands were ideal for this tropical tree. The cacao tree is very sensitive to the sun's rays, which can be harmful to the development of the cacao's fruit and seed. Therefore, larger shade trees are planted between the rows of cacao trees. In Cameroon, banana and plantain trees are used for shading the cacaos. Since the fruit of both trees is edible, putting banana and plantain trees between the cacao trees serves a double purpose.

Coffee is Cameroon's second most valuable cash crop. Coffee grows on the cooler slopes of the country's hills. Wild

The new Sanaga River dam brings increased electrical power to much of the country.

CAMEROON MINISTRY OF INFORMATION AND TOURISM

This rocky slope is part of the terraced farmland of the Gwoza people, who live in the mountains.

coffee bushes have always grown in the Sanaga River region. Early attempts to cultivate these wild bushes failed. But as farmers learned more about horticulture, they were able to cultivate these wild bushes and export their beans.

Rubber trees also grow wild in Cameroon. Early European settlers in this area saw this tree as a potential cash crop. In later years, the trees were exploited for their rubber. Today rubber is the country's third most valuable export.

The world market is always fluctuating, and the price at which agricultural goods can be sold always varies. Thus, the price of cacao, coffee, and rubber are affected by conditions throughout the world. If, in one year, the world-market price for these products is low or the crops fail, the country's profits are low. Cameroon realizes that it is not good to rely so heavily on only a few exports for its income, so it is trying to add more and different cash crops to its economy.

OTHER AGRICULTURE

Cotton has always grown wild in the northern sections of Cameroon. In attempts to make use of this cotton, a variety of improved cotton seeds were recently introduced. With modern farming methods, the cotton can now be cultivated. The cotton is now exported as a raw product. Some cotton is manufactured into cloth, and the cloth is exported.

Palm oil has also been cultivated for more than a century. Palm trees grow wild in Cameroon. They have long provided food by-products for the local people, who use palm oil in cooking and for making candles, lamp oil, wine, and soap. The Germans established palm-oil plantations in the colonial period. Many of these are now managed by the Cameroon Development Corporation, a government agency.

Many other food crops are grown only for local consumption. Two major staples (basic foods) are bananas and plantains. Another major staple, grown and used extensively for local use, is cassava, a root crop. Millet and maize are also important foods, and they are grown throughout the country.

WORKING ON AGRICULTURE

In addition to increasing the number of cash crops, the government is also trying to involve more people in agricultural work. Since few people can afford to own plantations, cooperatives are being

UNITED NATIONS

Women husking yellow corn.

organized. In a cooperative, a group of farmers work an area of land, producing a large volume of crops and sharing the profits. A cooperative can make small-scale farming profitable without destroying village life.

The "Peasant Plan" has been a part of Cameroon's Second Five-Year Plan for economic development. Under this plan, attempts have been made to provide land to the landless. These new landowners are also being taught how to work their land. If this plan works, the people in this program will not only grow enough food to satisfy their own basic needs, but they will also have a surplus of crops. They can sell this surplus through the cooperative associations, thus adding to the nation's cash economy. The government expects that this program will greatly increase the country's per capita (average for every individual) income.

Livestock has been raised successfully in the highlands and the savannas for many years. But the people raise it for their own needs. Meat for urban dwellers still must be imported. The government hopes to increase its livestock production to feed urban people. For the same reason, the government also hopes to increase the fishing industry, which is located both on the coast and in the country's many rivers.

Cameroon's forests contain extensive stands of valuable hardwoods. More than one-third of the country is forested. But the nation has not been able to utilize much of the raw forest materials because its transportation systems are too limited to bring the wood out of the forests. The government is also concerned with conserving these resources. In its conservation effort, the government has limited the number of licenses it issues to commercial lumber companies. These companies are required to plant a new tree to replace every one they remove. It is hoped that these and other measures will prevent the wasteful exploitation of the country's natural resources.

INDUSTRIAL DEVELOPMENT

Of all the French-speaking nations in Africa, Cameroon ranks third (after Ivory Coast and Senegal) in its industrial

Livestock at a tapki, *or artificial reservoir, near Bama.*

development. Light-industrial plants have been built, including a number of food-processing plants. At Garoua, in the north, are several food-processing factories that can and preserve meat bought from local cattle and livestock herders. At Kribi, along the coast, are a number of fish-processing plants. With great quantities of local grains available, some flour and bakery products are produced. Palm-oil products are manufactured at Victoria and Edea. These industries provide employment for many local people. The processing factories also enable canned and frozen foods to be made available in areas of the country where fresh foods cannot be found.

In Douala and other cities are a number of sawmills, plywood factories, and furniture factories. Recently, Cameroon has had a paper shortage. Thus, the government allowed an Austrian company to build a huge paper mill in Cameroon. The company will produce paper and paper products using eucalyptus trees. Although it will take a few years to establish the mill, Cameroon's paper problems should end when it is built.

There has been little development of heavy industry in Cameroon. The country

Logs are sometimes brought out of the forests by fleets of trucks.

The government has built many metal-roofed structures to provide better market sites. Merchants display their wares on rows of concrete-block counters.

needs to develop transportation before it can fully utilize known natural resources or explore for new ones. Probably Cameroon's largest heavy industry is the Alucam Industrial Complex at Edea. Here aluminum is made from bauxite ore (imported from Guinea) with the hydroelectric power of the Edea Falls. Local deposits of bauxite ore in Cameroon will be used to expand this operation when more roads or railroads are built.

TRADE

Cameroon's economy fluctuates yearly, due to the varying world-market prices of cacao, coffee, and rubber. Thus, it is hard for the government to predict what its

revenues from exports will be. Fortunately, the nation's balance of trade has been favorable in recent years.

While Cameroon exports mostly farm products, it imports manufactured goods and equipment needed for its agricultural development. Some food items, beverages, tobacco, and fuel are also imported.

About 70 percent of Cameroon's trade is with the EEC (European Economic Community), of which Cameroon is an associate member. Cameroon also cooperates with its neighbors in many trade agreements and associations. The country trades most often with other former French-African nations.

OIL

To develop an extensive transportation system requires a great deal of money. In order to earn the needed money, Cameroon hopes to capitalize on the expected wealth of its offshore oil. Presently, however, the oil deposits thought to be present have not been tapped.

Rich oil deposits have been worked in Gabon to the south and in Nigeria to the west. Cameroon has full confidence that it has oil worth tapping. Thus, the government has been pressing major oil companies, mainly foreign, to develop its oil deposits. Presently, Cameroon must import much oil from its neighbors and pay a high price for it. Some officials in Cameroon are concerned that the oil companies are merely holding the country's oil fields

Right: Cameroon's telecommunications system is constantly being improved. Here a Cameroonian technician (right) discusses a problem with a United Nations adviser. Below: Another United Nations adviser (right) assists a Cameroonian printer in bookbinding.

Residents of Bamendankwe build a bridge. They contribute one day each week for community development.

as a reserve supply for the future. There is great debate over this issue in Cameroon.

TRANSPORTATION

The lack of adequate transportation networks throughout Cameroon greatly affects the country's economic development. The mobility of the people is also greatly restricted. There are no good transportation routes that link East and West Cameroon or that link north and south. People in northern Cameroon often travel on the rivers into Nigeria, then use Nigerian transportation to reach the sea. In some areas of rural Cameroon, people must use transportation in the Central African Republic or Gabon in order to reach other parts of their own country.

In the 1930s, the road system built by the French in Cameroon was considered the best in equatorial Africa. But it has been expanded little since then. The road system is inadequate for today's needs. Only about nine hundred miles of paved roads exist, thirty-two hundred miles of secondary roads, and more than seventy-four hundred miles of other roads. But most of these roads are subject to seasonal conditions. During the rainy season, many roads are impassable.

A railway links Douala on the coast with Yaounde in the highlands, but it is quite old. About two hundred miles long, its construction dates back to the German and French colonial periods. In 1974 the government acquired a 16-million-dollar loan from the World Bank to improve a twenty-mile stretch of this railway. The track will be replaced, bridges constructed, and many new railroad cars purchased.

Also under construction is a Trans-Cameroon Railway, which will eventually link the coast with the northern interior. The railroad will also connect to railroads in Chad and the Central African Republic.

Air transportation in Cameroon, as in many other African nations, provides the fastest and most efficient way to get from place to place. Air travel is little affected by seasonal changes. Eighteen airports link the nation. Cameroon National Airlines provides flights to all of the smaller airports in the country. The international airport at Douala provides service for the country's national airlines, as well as for a number of major international airlines.

Sea traffic continues to be one of Cameroon's important means of transportation. Major port facilities at Douala service ships from all over the world. Kribi, in the south, has been developing its harbor and will soon be more suited to heavy-tonnage sea freight traffic than the harbor at Douala. Smaller-craft ports are also located at Tiko.

With inadequate transportation networks to provide direct contact between people, radio serves as the country's main form of communication. The government uses radio extensively to keep the people informed of the country's development and of national events. Many international and national magazines and newspapers are read by people in the major cities.

Enchantment of Cameroon

MOUNT CAMEROON

Rising from the range of mountains along the coast is Mount Cameroon, more than thirteen thousand feet high. Driving up the mountain's slopes, cool breezes from the Atlantic overtake the warm, sticky, humid air below. The pleasant climate of this mountain attracted British and German colonists years ago. On Mount Cameroon, colonists built their homes and established their colonial capital of Buea. Today Buea is the capital of the state of West Cameroon.

Mount Cameroon overlooks the Atlantic Ocean and the distant island of Fernando Po. Often the view is blocked by thick haze, formed by the combination of dense humidity and cool ocean breezes. Dark clouds cluster around the peak, and rain pours down the mountainside. The rainwater runs rapidly, downhill, flowing into streams and falling over rapids and waterfalls. Animals frequently must race to escape the storms.

Mount Cameroon offers exciting climbing. With rain forests, wild animals and birds, and countless streams and waterfalls, the scenery is beautiful. The climb is not severe, and a good hiker can scale the slope in two to three days.

THE COAST

Near Mount Cameroon is Douala. With

The marketplace at Yaounde. The clothing market is in the background.

Above: These children are playing telephone, a favorite game all over the world. Opposite: The big and busy port of Douala.

a population of 250,000, Douala is the largest city in the country. Factories and modern buildings adorn the city. Douala is the industrial hub of Cameroon, for it is here that all plane, train, and boat routes converge.

Along the coast near Douala are long stretches of white, sandy beaches lined with palm trees. The local people enjoy both bathing and fishing year round. The coastal towns of Victoria and Kribi have also retained their beautiful beaches, while still developing as modern towns.

THE NORTH

Because the country's transportation is still undeveloped, the far north and south are each relatively isolated. The predominantly Christian south is quite different from the predominantly Muslim north.

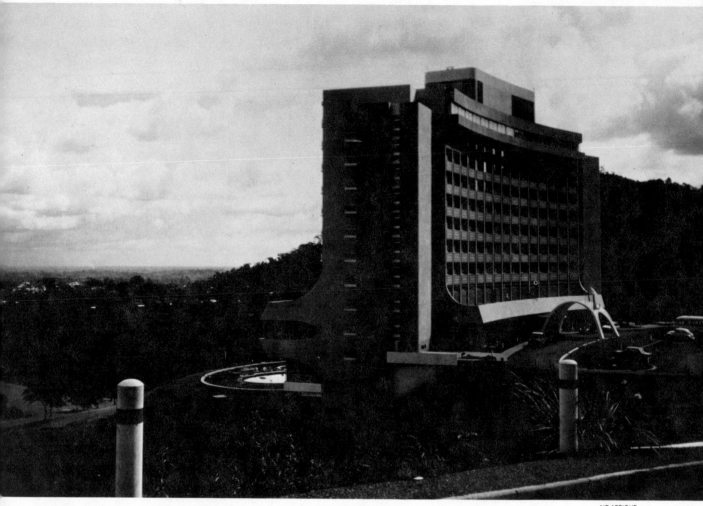

The new and modern Mont Febe Hotel overlooks the hills of Yaounde.

The cultural contrasts are striking, but the land is also different. The south is closer to the equator, more tropical, and closed in with rain forests. The north, on the other hand, is open savanna country dotted with broad-leaved trees.

Cameroon's largest game reserve is the Waza Game Reserve in the north. Many wild animals and birds inhabit this open savanna. Giraffes, antelope, elephants, and leopards still wander the area along their annual migration routes.

YAOUNDE

Yaounde is the country's rapidly growing capital city. Downtown Yaounde has a cosmopolitan atmosphere much like other major cities in the world. Theaters, restaurants, clothing stores, and shops all add to the city's modern feeling. The National Assembly building and other government buildings are open to the public. Yaounde's African Cultural Center houses some of the country's artworks. The University of Cameroon is located in this city of 120,000 people.

Yaounde's local markets still reflect the feeling of traditional rural markets. Local villagers bring their families, produce, and livestock to Yaounde on market day.

Colorful stalls are lined with merchants standing behind and umbrellas overhead. Some merchants sit on the ground, their produce neatly laid out on a cloth on the ground in front of them. Children, goats, and dogs run around among the stalls, sometimes knocking down or even snatching some food. A merchant yells at the culprit as he sneaks away.

The excitement on market day is overwhelming, and the brightness of the colors cannot be equaled. A spirit of friendship and hospitality can always be observed at the market.

Handy Reference Section

INSTANT FACTS

Political:

Official Name—United Republic of Cameroon

Form of Government—Republic

Capital—Yaounde

Monetary Unit—CFA franc

Official Languages—French and English

Independence Day—January 1

Main Political Party—Cameroon National Union

Flag—Tricolor (left to right) of green, red, and yellow vertical stripes, with two gold stars in the green stripe. Stars represent the states of West and East Cameroon.

National Anthem—"O Cameroon, Land of Our Ancestors"

Geographical:

Area—183,381 square miles

Highest Point—13,360 feet (Mount Cameroon)

Lowest Point—sea level

Administrative Regions	*Largest City*
Coastal	Douala
Eastern	Batouri
Northern	Maroua
South Central	Yaounde
West Cameroon	Bamenda
Western	Foumban

POPULATION

Population—5.7 million (estimate)

Growth Rate—2.2 percent

YOU HAVE A DATE WITH HISTORY

5th century B.C.—Hanno writes about Mount Cameroon's eruption

3rd century B.C.—Knowledge of iron-working probably comes to Cameroon

1472—Fernao de Po visits Cameroon coast

mid-1600s—Slave trade begins at Douala

1807—Britain declares slave trade illegal

1858—Albert Saker establishes missionary colony at Victoria

1884—Germans sign treaty with Douala king; colony of Kamerun established

1914—Douala send representative to Germany; Germans hang King Manga Bell

1919—Germany surrenders rights to Kamerun; League of Nations divides colony between France and Britain

1945—Cameroon-Cameroun put under British and French trusteeships

1955—"Bamileke Rebellion" breaks out

1958—U.N. General Assembly votes to end French trusteeship

1960—East Cameroon becomes independent nation (January 1); Ahmadou Ahidjo becomes president

1961—World Court rules election invalid (June 1); West Cameroon joins East Cameroon to form two-nation state (October 1)

1962—Two parties join into National Cameroon Union under President Ahidjo

1969—Ahidjo elected president of OAU

1972—Country renamed United Republic of Cameroon (May 20)

Index

93

About the Authors

With the publication of his first book for school use when he was twenty, **Allan Carpenter** began a career as an author that has spanned more than 135 books—with more still to be published in the Enchantment of Africa series for Childrens Press. After teaching in the public schools of Des Moines, Mr. Carpenter began his career as an educational publisher at the age of twenty-one when he founded the magazine *Teachers Digest*. In the field of educational periodicals, he was responsible for many innovations. During his many years in publishing, he has perfected a highly organized approach to handling large volumes of factual material: after extensive traveling and having collected all possible materials, he systematically reviews and organizes everything. From his apartment high in Chicago's John Hancock Building, Allan recalls: "My collection and assimilation of materials on the states and countries began before the publication of my first book." Allan is the founder of Carpenter Publishing House and of Infordata International, Inc., publishers of *Issues in Education* and *Index to U.S. Government Periodicals*. When he is not writing or traveling, his principal avocation is music. He has been the principal bassist of many symphonies, and he managed the country's leading non-professional symphony for twenty-five years.

Co-author **James W. Hughes** has traveled extensively through over half of the nations of Africa and lived and worked in Kenya for several years. Dr. Hughes has contributed to journals and books in both Africa and the United States. He has served as chairman of the International Activities Committee of the National Council for the Social Studies, and has served as an educational consultant for the International Relations Committee of the National Education Association in both Kenya and Nepal. Dr. Hughes is currently Director of Teacher Education at Oakland University.

967
C

CARPENTER

Cameroon

DATE DUE	BORROWER'S NAME	ROOM NO.
3-18-80	aileen, M.	28
OCT 2 5 1982	Mrs. Riehl	28
1-29-91	Kristina Taylor	T-13

967
C

CARPENTER

Cameroon